Christina Stewart

Copyright © 2013 by Christina Stewart.

Library of Congress Control Number:   2011913533
ISBN:         Hardcover      978-1-4836-6529-0
              Softcover      978-1-4836-6528-3
              Ebook          978-1-4836-6530-6

All rights reserved. No part of this book may be reproduced or transmitted in any form or by any means, electronic or mechanical, including photocopying, recording, or by any information storage and retrieval system, without permission in writing from the copyright owner.

Rev. date: 07/05/2013

**To order additional copies of this book, contact:**
Xlibris Corporation
0800-443-678
www.xlibris.co.nz
Orders@Xlibris.co.nz
700701

My personal journey in life due to many unique circumstances that have taken place has encouraged me to share my story. The Lord works in many mysterious ways and for many reasons that we do not understand at the time. My journey is beyond anything I ever imagined could be possible. The narrow path that we have to tread is made up of many steps as we journey and our individual experiences shape and make up who and what we are.

I now understand as I mature in years and in faith that we can truly trust our dear Lord to bring us through, God works for good for those who love him and we must learn to be content in all circumstances hard as that may be at times. We must live by faith and completely trust in the Son of God who loves us and gave himself up for us he will do anything to ensure that his loved ones have all the blessings and provisions for our every need according to the riches of his glory in Christ Jesus our Lord.

So I will begin to share my path on life's journey with you in a very personal way due to the love and trust of my relationship with Jesus as he has walked with me along the way. It took many long years for me to realise that I was journeying alongside him but I now know that he has always been there as the famous poem "footprints" says when I did not know he was there it was then that he carried me

# CHAPTER 1

My life began in April 1955. I was born into a loving family I was the middle child of three girls my elder sister three years older and much later seven years younger my other sister. I was born in the island of Lewis in the Western Isles of Scotland. This is a small island on the west coast with a population of around thirty thousand I recall a very pleasant upbringing we lived on a croft which is a piece of land around seven acres. Life then was very different from the present in those days the land was used we were totally self sufficient.

We had our own cow that provided all the milk we made our own butter and cheese. We had our own chickens that provided eggs and meat and also sheep. Baking was done most days bread scones and cakes, meat and fish was salted or dried, no freezers in those days! All the vegetables were grown and stacked up for the winter the pit was dug up vegetables put in and covered up with earth. Income for families was fishing and the weaving of the famous Harris Tweed. I remember the defined seasons then, which now seems to have disappeared long hot summers spent on the beaches and in contrast long cold winters wading through the snow. We even had our own fuel for the Winter the peat was cut in a special way and laid out in the sun to dry and then stacked up beside the houses to heat the homes in the cold season. Our first language was Gaelic which we all spoke fluently we learned English when we went to school at age five.

It was a very sheltered youth we had, times must have been hard but everyone was happy, worked very hard and shared companionship. I was raised in a very religious household as many families on the island were then. Anyone who knows the islands will be aware that they were, and some still are, steeped in traditional traditions that go back a very long way. I will not comment much on the traditions but just to say that now when I look back rituals and expectations where way over the top.

As children we were made to go to church every Sunday which was a sacred day there was no negotiation and it was not just once either. We went to church in the morning we had to walk as it was against the religion to drive on the Sunday and it was about a mile. We had to wear hats and coats and sit for nearly two hours without moving listening to a strict sermon which children were no part of I do not recall taking anything away from those services it was way over the top for children. We would walk home then off again to Sunday school in the afternoon I recall getting much more out of this at least there was some interaction. Then off again we would go in the evening same again to church for another two hour service if that was not enough we would then sit around the fireside reading and learning more about the bible. We were not allowed to go outside on Sunday apart from going to church I never understood what that was about and was extreme. In the island there was no public transport on Sunday no shops open life came to a total halt.

This was the ritual for the whole of my upbringing I do not blame my parents but this was extreme and overpowering, they were steeped in tradition and did what they thought was right and proper. Instead of encouragement on reflection at that time it had the opposite effect. Sunday was sacred nobody was to do anything except attend church and serve God it was extreme. Thankfully things have moved on since that time although some are still steeped in the old traditions most are now open to change.

Childhood continued we had a very sheltered upbringing we attended the local school in the village we had to walk to school every day and even sometimes walk home for lunch as well. I had always from a very young age expressed that I wanted to be a nurse so in order to get the qualifications necessary to do this had to go to the high school in the town seven miles away. When I went to the high school and started mixing with other teenagers from different places I somehow rebelled. I soon realised that our sheltered lifestyle as a family was not actually how everyone lived we were really naive there was another world out there to explore and boy was I going to do it. Our sheltered upbringing was not conducive to dealing with the big bad world. Do not get me wrong I do not blame anybody but myself for the decisions that I made but curiosity and experimenting was fun and exciting but I had to find out the very opposite the hard way.

# CHAPTER 2

In amongst my studies I discovered boys, fun, dancing at the weekends and smoking and drinking boy this was fun when I reflect now on those times and what I put my parents through it makes me very sad. I was a curious teenager finding my way in the adult world. Anyway towards the end of my two year studies and on the eve of my exams you will not believe it I was pregnant my whole world had collapsed. I had met the man who was to become my husband and the father of my children he was eight years older than me and was fun and exciting at the time. We would be out drinking and dancing every weekend I was getting free drinks in the local pub at Christmas for being a regular did I look that old! It was all bound to have ended in disaster on reflection and that was just what it was for me I did not sit my exams my chances were ruined there was no way back now what a disgrace and a disappointment I was.

The next hurdle then was how to tell my parents I had hid the secret for five months and I dreaded the outcome. I expected to be punished and rejected. My older sister was the one who broke the ice and revealed the secret and I was really surprised that everyone stood by me I did not deserve it. It was frowned upon in this culture and at that time but there was a huge price to pay I had to get married as this was thought to be the right and proper thing to do I was probably so relieved that it was all out in the open that I could not protest The wedding was promptly arranged and took place within a month.

Before the wedding I became very unwell with an infection in my kidneys I will never forget the pain of that I had very high temperatures and was delirious at times a wedding was the last thing on my mind. Deep down I knew it was not the right thing for me but what choice did I have I was very young and naive and went along with it, all I had to do was turn up on the day. The wedding took place in April 1972 five days after my seventeenth birthday.

We lived with my parents for a while after the wedding my husband inherited a house from his father but was very run down and needed a lot of work done to it. We did not have a lot of money my husband was a self employed weaver and worked from home we would eventually work on the house and move there eventually. This was not an easy time for anyone but I felt safe with my family around me and was a huge transition for me and my family.

On the morning of August 11$^{th}$ 1972 I awoke in the early hours of the morning in a lot of pain I thought my infection was back the pain was so intense I did not realise it but I was in advanced labour. This was so unlike anything that the text books tell you I could not identify contractions the pain was so constant I made my way to the hospital and within two hours I had given birth to a baby boy over eight pounds without so much as a paracetamol what a shock it was nothing like what I expected.

My whole world had changed and would never ever be the same again as I was handed this little bundle I now realised that I was a responsible mother I loved him immediately and named him Don Neil but I was also very scared. My son was the first baby and male child in the family for a long time and was loved and spoilt by everyone. I knew then that I was never going to achieve my ambition of being a nurse and I was devastated with that but that was the price I had to pay.

Life went on and I soon discovered that I was pregnant again and by this time we were getting closer to move to our own home we had slowly got it done to a state that we could move in soon. There were no luxuries no washing machine to start with cloth nappies were boiled on the stove top no disposable nappies then we had to save hard for everything we had. My daughter Mairi was born on 5$^{th}$ September 1973 again quickly and with no pain relief. Life was very busy with a house move and two young children and day to day living continued. We worked hard to make a good home and again I was pregnant, my second daughter Margaret was born in February 27$^{th}$ 1975. Here I was the mother of three children and still just under twenty I loved them all dearly and enjoyed every moment of motherhood my whole life revolved round my children it was a real blessing to have three healthy children but it was hard work. The children all grew up together and were very close I was with them the whole time as they grew up in the early years and never left them with anyone before they all went to school.

# CHAPTER 3

In the village we had good neighbours and I became very friendly with a new neighbour and we had children of the same age and they all grew up together. This woman's mother was the matron at one of the local hospitals on the island I got to know her well and she was aware of my desire to have always wanted to be a nurse. This very special woman was to become a mentor to me and became the greatest influence in my life in years to come and made my dream of becoming a nurse a reality. I owe this woman so much, a very gracious Christian woman whom I grew to love and admire and was sent into my life for a reason is God not good!

This woman was aware of my great passion to be a nurse, she took me under her wing, she sat me down and told me her plan for me and the future. The plan was that when my youngest child went to school she would give me a job at the hospital as a carer and that this would give me a sound background for nursing then when the children were old enough that I would go and do my nurse training. This was my guardian angel and was the start of my nursing journey I could not believe it that someone would think that I was still worthy of supporting my dreams I would be very happy to take up the carers job but to become a nurse I still did not believe that this would ever happen but this woman and someone else had other beliefs!

So sure enough the year that Margaret started school in 1980 this woman offered me a job I was able to take it up I had passed my driving test just before that and as my husband worked from home he was always there to look after the children when I was not there. I worked part time and mostly night shift which worked perfectly as I was able to sleep when the children were at school and never more than three days a week. I loved every minute of the job although it was hard work but loved mixing with colleagues and earning money which I had never done and doing what I always wanted to do.

We renovated the house in the next few years to a high standard and made it a good home we worked hard and it was all paid for life was busy and hectic. I did this job for ten years and then true to her word my mentor came and told me it was now time for me to go and do my nurse training by this time my youngest daughter was fifteen and both my daughters were nearly finishing high school my son was just about to leave home and commence an engineering cadetship with P and O shipping what a sad day that was when he left to go to the other side of the world at seventeen I cried buckets as he climbed onto the plane that day.

I had by now matured and I was ready for a challenge my children were pretty much independent and I had time for me at last but of course I was very apprehensive. As I had left school without the qualifications needed to commence my nurse training I had to sit a very stiff entrance exam but I did it and passed so I was accepted to commence my nurse training in January 1990 I would do eighteen months in Stornoway on the island and had to go to the mainland in Inverness to do the second half of the training.

At this time and for a long time before this me and my husband had drifted apart and there was not much between us by now. In the early days all our time was spent looking after the children but now that the children were older it was very different and it was then that I realised that there was actually very little left between us life and all it's business had drifted us along. My husband at this time had developed a dependence on drink, some people who may know him may not agree but if they do not then they do not know him at all. In my book he was an alcoholic, not a down and out but every weekend was an absolute nightmare for both me and the children he would start drinking on Friday and this would continue all weekend his worst day would be Sunday probably because he knew nobody would see him. Believe me I could write another book about this time and nobody would believe it, to the outside world he could be charming but inside the home he was impossible to live with. On reflection I do not know why or how I put up with it but again someone was looking after me. I do not wish to disclose here my nightmare but believe me that is exactly what it was I had become a mental wreck and I was like a piece of old wood broken and useless.

So to have been given this lifeline was just what I needed I had the potential to achieve my lifelong ambition to be a nurse I knew it would not be easy but I felt determined to achieve it. God sure was working in mysterious ways but I could not see that at the time but on reflection now I know it was all meant to be and there was always a purpose for it. I started training in January it was this very month that my youngest daughter

Margaret started having trouble with her joints when her knees started to dislocate this for her was her own personal journey and nightmare and led to many major operations and still continues for her but she herself has also now through all of her trials realised that God is in charge of her life which is comforting, no matter what happens in our lives if we have faith that is all that we will ever need. I enjoyed the challenge of my nurse training it was like a long term dream coming to reality.

# CHAPTER 4

Just prior to starting my training a few years before a new family had moved into the village and recently had started to socialise with the neighbours. Little did I know then that I had actually met the man that was to become my soulmate my very best friend and the man I was going to spend the very best part of my life with and whom I loved dearly and still do and always will. This man was called Alasdair I did not take much heed of him initially but as I got to know him more I discovered someone who had the unique gift of been a great listener be non judgemental and to give amazing advice.

Alasdair was aware of my home situation and saw for himself on many occasions what I had to put up with. As I got to spend time with him I found I could easily talk with him and reveal all my worries and concerns he became like a buddy to me and I found this so therapeutic. I also listened to him and found that he himself had a tragic story to tell he had been married and had two daughters when the children were just five and seven they were all involved in a car accident and his wife was killed he was left to bring the children up on his own and had now moved to the village. I now know I had to meet this man it was all meant to be.

I continued with my nurse training eighteen months of hard slog working full time doing shift work and also looking after a family and also studying for exams it was not easy. The long hours and some very late nights was hard but for me it was worth it as I was trying to achieve my ambition. I did not share the unrest in my marriage with anyone but the drinking was getting worse and only those that were very close to me were aware. During this time I continued to get closer to Alasdair and he became my very best friend he could see how much I was hurting If I brought up the subject with my husband he would make out that it was me that had a problem it certainly was not him! I moved to Inverness in September 1991 to finish the rest of my training by this time I had become closer than ever to Alasdair I kept in touch with him and he gave me so much encouragement to finish my training he knew how much it all meant to me.

I did not feel proud of what was happening I was getting involved with another man who by then I knew was getting to be more than just a friend and cared for him deeply and he for me. Why was this happening to me I could not understand it I knew I was not happy but I never thought this would ever happen but it was just as if it was all meant to be and had no control over it. I was still married and mother of three children I was hopefully going to achieve my dream of becoming a nurse what a situation to be in and what to do about it. It was after I moved away from home that I truly realised that sure there was another world out there my goodness the peace and quiet and tranquillity no more drunken episodes every weekend it was another world I did not need this hassle in my life again I did feel guilty leaving the girls at home but they were now old enough to care for themselves.

I knew definitely by then in my subconscious that I was definitely in the wrong situation my marriage was dead but I did not think for one moment that it would change or that I would ever get out of it. Alasdair and I kept in touch we did not share what was happening with anyone at that time I would return to the island from time to time when I had days off I had many conversations with my husband stating it was all over but of course he would not believe that I would ever do anything about it deep down he knew it too but his trump card was that I would never do it how could I let my parents down again and what a disappointment I would be to them again he knew that this would be the hardest thing ever for me to do.

Anyway I did manage to finish my training and in April 1993 I graduated as a RGN six students started in the class and only two of us graduated that day and I was one of them! I was ecstatic and my mentor the very woman that made it all possible for me told me she was as proud of me that day as if I was her own daughter she told me she always knew I could and would make it I loved this woman more than ever.

# CHAPTER 5

Then again amazing things started to happen to me. I had finished my training I had been doing my last two modules in Raigmore hospital there were some jobs coming up and I was told to apply as I had been there for six months and got to know them well. I applied as any job after qualifying is worth taking to gain experience. I did not hear anything and was preparing to go back to the island I went to the ward to say farewell and to give a little gift I met the nurse who had been my mentor and she asked me when my interview was I told her that I did not have one she was amazed and told me that I was picked and that she was going to get in touch with the charge nurse. In the next couple of days I had a phone call to attend an interview. So how amazing was that if I had not gone to the ward that very day I would never have had that interview and I would have returned back to the island. I had the interview and got a job I was very happy I call it fate but it proves that there is someone else in charge and taking care of our lives and shaping it for us he sure does have a plan for our journey in the background.

I got a job that was initially part time but soon became full time I was not going back home the decision had been made for me I enjoyed gaining experience in a busy ward and all was well for now anyway. I moved to another wing of the nurses homes and moving in the same day was another girl who lived in Inverness but was also from the island and who became a very good friend. This woman had split up with her husband and was starting out on her own we were together there for nearly two years we became close and had many long conversations in that time.

Life went on and then Alasdair decided that he would move to Inverness my goodness was he doing this for me he told me no he had not really settled in the island the children had grown up and his younger daughter had actually started her nurse training by now and he also had four sisters living in Inverness. We were very close by now and it did not seem right I was still married although in name only but it was as if I had no control over it, it was just happening.

My flatmate started looking at moving and buying her own place and looked at getting a morgage in a kind of way I was jealous that she had made that decision and was secretly thinking if I could or would ever be able to do it or would get the courage to be in that position. My reasoning was telling me that it was such a hard thing to do and did not think it would ever happen to me. Then suddenly my father became unwell and passed away I was gutted my father had been a huge support and encouragement to me in my training.

# CHAPTER 6

I felt under some pressure to return to the island but again decisions were made that were outwith my control and something mysterious happened to confirm to me that someone else was in charge of the situation. I had word from one of the charge nurses where I had worked for years while I was a carer that a job was coming up and to apply for it she told me I would get the job all I had to do was come to the interview. I had very mixed emotions about it part of me was happy that she thought that I was worthy of the job and part of me was sad I did not deep down want to go back to live there.

It was Alasdair again who encouraged me to go and told me that if it was meant to be that it would happen and if it was not meant that there was a reason for that as well and that it would all work out the way it was meant to. So off I went to the interview I was met and told that the charge nurse from the ward could not be there as her husband had a heart attack that morning and her place would be taken by a charge nurse from another ward. Wow—how was this happening how incredible was this anyway I did not get the job it was not meant to be someone was again making the decisions for me behind the scenes it was out of our control I can not say I was disappointed.

I returned to the mainland and continued with my job one weekend started talking about her friend who had been to see a clairvoyant and had an amazing experience she herself was keen to go and asked me if I would go with her I said yes so she made an appointment for us both. So off we went one evening this woman lived out in the country in an old farm house. What an experience that turned out for me.

We arrived at the house she did the readings in the top room of the house I stayed downstairs my friend had the first reading it felt like a very long time before she came down. Anyway now it was my turn, we climbed the stairs to a small room the light were dim and there was tarot cards and a crystal ball on the table we sat opposite each other across the table. I had made a conscious decision before we left that I would take off my rings I did not want this woman to know anything about me or to have any signs to go by. This woman told me to shuffle the tarot cards I glanced across the table and she had her eyes closed and appeared to be meditating when she opened her eyes she looked straight at me and told me to hold both her hands. She looked straight at me and said "my dear you are hurting so much, you have come here for an answer tonight and I hope that I can help you I do not know how you can get up in the mornings and face the world the way you are feeling you are stuck in a very bad relationship and I want to let you know now that you are going to get out of it"

To hear this I was thoroughly amazed and I could feel goose bumps all over me how did she know this and how right was she!! Then she closed her eyes again and said that there was a presence in the room she said it was someone that had passed to the other side and cared for me and was sending me lots of love and his name is Alex. She asked me if I knew who this was I said no I did not know anyone by that name she told me it could be someone from way back but he was definitely here. So she said what else can we make from this name maybe Alexander or Sandy oh my goodness again I could feel the goose bumps Of course I knew Sandy this was my brother in law who had died he was in the merchant navy and was lost at sea in January and they did not find his body until April

Thank goodness she said the presence is so real he is in the room and sends you all his love. This to me was nearly unbelievable but it did not feel uncomfortable at all she went on to say that he was surrounded by water and so many flowers was it around this time it was within a week of the anniversary of his burial I was amazed by all this but there was more to come. She then told me that I was going to get out of this bad relationship that I was in I thought to myself no way that will never happen but she went on to say I assure you that it will happen "one day you will wake up and without any thought it will just happen"

Then she went on to say "I can see them all in the island sitting gossiping because that is what they do but do not worry they will soon find something else to talk about" I could imagine that all right but she went on to say that they would be judging me but after all they did not know the truth I was the only one that did, how true. She told me that it would all take time but eventually every person that meant anything to me would stand by me I could not believe what I was hearing.

If that was not enough this woman then told me that I had already met a very special man, WOW, this was too much the words that she used were "this is like a marriage made in heaven and we would be very happy" my goodness I was blown away how on earth did she know this? She told me that I would travel a lot with this man she told me about his wife and the accident it was all too much to take in. She continued to tell me that I would get a new home she said a house with roses round the door and that I would know when I saw it she said times will be hard but you will get through it that I would never have lots of money but that I would always have enough. She told me that I was very close to the spirits and to speak to them when they came to visit I was spooked she said that they all loved me. When we came back down the stairs she said to my friend that I had an amazing experience that she never had and that I was soon going to have a very stressful time coming up and that I would need her support. So off home we went as I was telling my friend all that she told me she was also amazed there was very little sleep that night I can tell you.

# CHAPTER 7

My flatmate a short while later had been to the mortgage shop she was ready to move on we got talking and we both had enough of living in nurses homes she said to me to go and see if I also could get a mortgage I told her that I would find out the next time I was in town. So next day off I did go into town and did go in to enquire the woman in the shop was very helpful and told me that she did not see any problem with me getting a mortgage I told her that at this stage I was just enquiring she told me to fill in the forms anyway and if I did decide to go ahead then it would be on file. We began to fill in the forms marital status she said separated I said as soon as the word came out of my mouth I froze why did I say that? I was not separated but I could not go back on what I had said it was said and done now. We finished filling in the rest of the forms in a daze I could not get out of that shop quick enough.

I took a deep breath and started walking into town and made for the first phone booth I could find, there were no mobile phones then, and I phoned my daughters and told them that I today had made a decision and was going to separate and start out on my own they both initially said that I had said this before and not gone through with it but I told them what had happened and they then realised that I was serious about this. So just as the clairvoyant had said that I would get up one day and that it would just happen that is exactly how it was that word separated was somehow placed in my mouth again I was amazed he sure does work in mysterious ways.

So the next step was to go to the island and face the music I did this at the first opportunity I told my husband my intention and again he did not believe that I was serious and again playing his trump card how was I going to tell my mother I told him that however hard it was going to be that I was going to do it. I still did not think that I would do it but I had now grown up I had found that there was another world out there without any hassles and I had served my sentence in this place and I was determined to go through with it after all that had happened I truly believe it was all meant to be.

    I went to see my mother I knew this was going to be the hardest thing ever I had a chat with her and told her of my plans I did not know how she was going to take it but I needed have worried. I was amazed at her reaction she told me that she already knew that things were not good I broke down and became very emotional at last it was all out in the open my Mum was so sad that I had to go through all this and told me that it would all work out it was not the reaction I expected. I came back to the home really upset I was devastated I felt I was a real failure of course my husband was amazed that I had actually done it his words were "I told you it would be that hard" but I think the biggest disappointment for him was that I had actually done it and now there was no way back. The next reaction was how could I have done this to him he had done nothing wrong well if that is what he thought then he sure was sick but I kept strong and stuck with it.

# CHAPTER 8

I returned to Inverness I had walked away with just my bag and just a few personal items that were of sentimental value to me I left him with the home which was all paid for a car in the garage and no debts never would I ever be accused of taking his precious house I had slogged my guts out to make this home and had to endure what I had to endure and let me say nobody will ever know it all you will never ever have a clue how bad it was at times but I was just happy to let him have it although I was entitled to half of it all I was glad to walk away with nothing. I had served my sentence and was now free my children were independent and whatever happened to me now I could start again from scratch hard as that was going to be but I would have been happy in a cardboard box as long as I never had that turmoil in my life again.

Then I started looking for property when I got back I did not have any money so I needed a one a one hundred per cent mortgage I spent a few weeks looking and could not really find anything suitable of course I did not have a car so it had to be within walking distance or on a good bus route to work. Eventually I found a really nice semi detached house near the hospital it was been sold by a nurse who worked at the hospital she was getting married and moving in to her husband's place This home was immaculate and did not need any work I put in an offer and was accepted. You won't believe it but she asked me if I would be interested in buying any of the furniture which was all very nice and good quality I told her I could not afford it but she said I could have it and to pay her back as I was able I could not believe this was happening someone sure was taking care of me. I was able to take the furniture and was able to pay her back in a few months all I had to do was move in and not worry.

I could not believe my luck I now owned my little home and it was all mine although it was going to be a long hard struggle no more worries what an achievement. I could walk to work and best of all Alasdair lived just down the road and you will not believe this but there was three rose bushes under the living room window and a climbing rose by the front door just like the woman had said you will get a house with roses round the door more amazing things.

I continued to work hard and it was a financial struggle at times but I can say that I was never overdrawn in the bank one month I had twenty seven pence in my bank account but I managed I had to pinch myself at times I could not believe that I had done it. This was the hardest thing I ever had to do in my life I felt like a failure and I had lost a lot of weight and felt unworthy of anything. I was not attending church at all I was very far from any faith and was life a piece of wood withered and worn. I had failed miserably in life in many aspects and claimed that I was an atheist I found it very hard at that time to believe in anything but on reflection is was just all that I had been through I was low in mood and struggling to come to terms with my life.

It was again Alasdair who walked alongside me encouraging me and offering support he was always there for me never ever pushing me but just quietly supporting me in any decisions I made he was my rock to which I clung to for sheer survival. What a very special man that was sent into my life again the Lord was working in very special ways we often later in life discussed how we were always meant to be together and the journey for us both was determined.

I throughout all this turmoil was still determined to do further study so I enroled with the Open University and I obtained a diploma in health and social welfare which I finished in 1997 then I was determined to also study for a degree that had been my goal I wanted to do it for me just to prove to myself that I was not stupid although I had stuffed up in many aspects and life did not work out the way I wanted I was determined to do it. I was working in Oncology and Haematology a busy ward and what a special place this turned out to be I knew by then that this was my chosen career and so I started to study for my degree which was taught at Marie Curie centre in Glasgow and in conjunction with Napier University in Edinburgh. I will not pretend and say it was easy it was sheer hard work doing full time shift work and also trying to study and also travel from time to time to Glasgow for study days. There were many many late nights trying to finish essays but I persevered and I did finish and got my degree in 2005 what an achievement that was I now had a Bsc in Cancer and Palliative care. I was proud of myself just shows what determination can do.

# CHAPTER 9

As I was getting settled in my new world financially I was more stable then me and Alasdair started travelling I had never been out of the coutry before so this was a great adventure for me and was the start of many wonderful holidays we were hooked soon as we came back we would be making plans for the next trip and sometimes we would go abroad twice in one year. Both our families were now accepting of our relationship we did keep it secret for a while we were not proud of what had happened but we both knew that it was meant to be. I once said to a friend that I had regretted that I had stayed in an unhappy relationship for such a long time and had spent the best part of my life in that situation she corrected me by saying "no it was not the best part of your life just the longest" how right she was and I never forgot it the best part of my life was now and the times to come. Just like the clairvoyant had said that we would travel lots and that everyone would be accepting.

We continued to love life and each other I was by now a senior nurse in Oncology and Haematology in the local hospital and it was during my time here that I truly learnt who and what I really was and what life was all about it was a very special place and a very special time in my journey. New things were happening we got the status of the cancer centre of the highlands in Scotland and I was proud to be part of it jobs were coming and going and then into my life came a very special person she had come from working in Edinburgh her name was Rhoda she was from the island but I had never met her before she turned out to become my very best friend and we had many happy times and many adventures together. In this special place we looked after many special people over the fifteen years that I worked there but it was in the beginning that were the real special times what a great team of people and what special people it was here that I also met Iain who was the chaplain at the time and who was a very special man we spent many years working together and I truly believe that we made a huge difference to people's lives that were in our care.

At this stage I still had not been attending church I still thought that I had no beliefs at all but God had other ideas which was soon to enfold I was going to have a significant experience that brought me back to believe in a very special way. My friend Rhoda was a Christian of many years but she did not push me at all in any way and also Iain used to come to the ward regularly and we cared for very special people in the course of our work. I believe that Gods presence was very evident in that place at that time and many amazing things happened. One day I was looking after a woman who was near death and had made peace the chaplain had visited on many occasions and she was ready and was now pretty much unconscious this evening her husband went away for a short break and I stayed with her shorty after she raised her arm and started waving beyond and said "Jean I am coming" I was amazed by this gesture and when I told her husband when he came back he was equally amazed he then told me that when they first got married that they had a still born child and they had named her Jean.

I was spooked and started reflecting on this and began to think how I could ever doubt that there was another life to come I believed this happened for a reason and was the start of my awakening This woman passed away in the night and I had a very strong urge to go to her funeral which we did not always do but I felt that I needed to be there I asked Rhoda if she would come with me of course she said she would. Iain was taking the service along with her own minister Iain read from Ecclesiastes chapter three, there is a time for everything and I do believe that it was a time for me. When we came out I said to Rhoda that I had never heard that before she told me a long time later that she knew then that I was on a journey and of course that I heard this before but I had never heard it the way I did then.

By this time in my journey both my daughters were married and leading their own lives my son had a girlfriend but not married then although he did marry later on my two daughters never left the island but my son never came back to live there after he left he was now in Glasgow on the mainland of Scotland. Work was busy and there was some major change about to happen we were going to split and move to another ward so the charge nurse at that time organised for six nurses of different grades and herself to attend a three day course with a trained facilitator on how to manage this change. We were very honoured this was to take place in a very nice hotel about an hours drive from Inverness we would be resident there the whole time and I was one of them and so was Rhoda this took place in August 2000.

So off we went on a Monday morning we would be there until Wednesday night when we arrived the facilitator set out the programme of the week we would be attending workshops in the day and then after dinner at night we would be watching a movie that was chosen by her and we were also told to keep a diary each day as we went on so that we could reflect on it at the end of the day. Soon after arrival we started the workshops and we all enjoyed the day that evening we watched the movie called The Doctor which was a movie about a consultant that had cancer and was very thought provoking after the movie we met up and had a few drinks together we each had our own rooms and when I went to my room to retire I started to write in my diary of what the day meant to me I wrote some and then tried to get some sleep but sleep would not come tried everything but I just could not get to sleep and I was wide awake the whole night I started writing in the diary again and went to breakfast the next day with no sleep not even five minutes.

I had written in my diary how my experience on the ward had been like the doctor in the movie the doctor had cancer of the larynx and now had no voice and that is what I felt that there was no voice left after all the stresses that had been happening I had written powerful stuff and I don't know where it came from it just seemed to flow from the pen. Anyway the next day we started the workshops again I felt fine but tired. The facilitator asked if anyone wanted to share their diary I said that I would so I stood up and started reading in a very strong and emotional way what I had written the night before at the end I broke down and walked out of the room Rhoda followed me out and said to me "Christina that was the most powerful thing ever where did that come from?" I told her that I did not know where it came from and that it was so unlike me I did not know what was happening to me but I had somehow lost control.

This was the start of a very amazing journey for me that carried on for over a week or more I was not able to take much more part in the workshops I became very confused and was fluctuating between mania and confusion what had happened to me I had no control over anything That second night after dinner we were to watch the film called Life is Beautiful and everyone had settled down to watch the movie I remained disturbed and remember the start of the movie then out of the blue I raised both arms and said "it is over we have won" my goodness where did that come from. The facilitator asked if I had seen the movie before no I had not but anyone that has seen this movie will know that those are the closing words of the movie my goodness what was happening here.

A couple of years later Rhoda found the movie and we both watched it together and it made so much sense to me then it is a story about the power of love and the human spirit during the war in order to survive a young boy had unconditional love and faith in his father in order to be saved and that was exactly the journey that I was on as well at that time but it did not end there.

# CHAPTER 10

I again went to bed that night and again I could not sleep I just did not know what was happening to me one minute I seemed fine and the next minute confused and out of control. I was unable to take any more part in the workshops and the next day the charge nurse took me home they thought that maybe I would be able to sleep in my own bed. I was very unstable and knew I was not right. I got in touch with Alasdair when I got home and he was shocked to see me back so early and to see the state I was in I had been absoloutly fine when I left two days before. I was in the bedroom trying to get some sleep but sleep would not come much we spent some time chatting then out of the blue Alasdair said to me "I think I know what is wrong with you I have seen this before" I think if you start reading the bible you might get some answers there he said that I was on a spiritual journey. I don't know why he said that but at that time I could not remember or know what I was doing or saying.

So I did as Alasdair had said and started reading in the bible and for the first time it was starting to make sense to me and I could relate to it in a very big way I could not put the book down this was amazing. I wrote down verses that really were significant and I still have this list in my bible to this day on the other side of the world. Of special signifigance was Galatians chapter six verse seven, Mark chapter four, John charter sixteen, John chapter six verse sixty three and also psalm ninty nine.

I still continued to fluctuate and had some confusing times but I had no control over it whatsoever I knew I was not right we had booked a holiday well before this and we were going to Malta for two weeks and we were due to leave that Friday Alasdair decided we should still go I just went along with it and trusted his judgement. So off we went I think there were some hairy moments along the way I only remember parts of it Alasdair often told me that I did not need to be told everything so there must have been some stressful moments for him. Anyway we arrived there and I still was not right the whole weekend I was fluctuating still and on Sunday I just got up from the dining table and Alasdair found me sitting on the floor at the room he was frustrated and so was I what was going on I knew I needed help and so Alasdair said that he was going to contact a doctor on Monday morning little did I know then what was ahead of me.

# CHAPTER 11

The doctor came to assess me in the morning and the next thing I was to be admitted to hospital for further assessment I was admitted to a private hospital that was very nice and modern I can only really remember small episodes of it but I do remember that they were trying to give me intravenous fluids and I was having none of it I was very disturbed and two people were brought in to special me that night and Alasdair also stayed in the room I don't think I slept much that night. The next morning it was decided that I would be transferred to another hospital I remember waiting in the courtyard for the ambulance to arrive I was going to St Luke's hospital and what a dump that was after the posh place I had just left. I remember that the doctor was from Scotland originally what a small world and I remember getting a chest x ray and an ECG and then there was some concern that I had some cardiac condition and was commenced on medication. I had in the past had some abnormal ECGs but never had any chest pain before. I remember lying in a bed in a scant room on my own and was in a catatonic state I would not move and would not eat or drink and would not speak.

It was decided that they would send for Alasdair as he had gone back to the hotel for a break and I remember just lying on the bed and suddenly I had come out of my body and I was hovering above the bed suspended in the air I was trying desperately to get back into my body but I could not. Then I heard voices speaking to me and the voices were saying to me that I was never going back into that body but that if I acknowledged Christ as my saviour that then I would get back but it would be to a new body. It was not a dream and it felt very surreal anyway after a while I drifted back into my body. Well, talk about birth and been reborn I had actually physically experienced it whether this was all spiritual entirely or was a near death experience where I actually died or both I don't know but all I know is that it did happen and was very real.

I still remained disturbed and it was decided that I would be transferred again to another hospital this was a psychiatric hospital and it was called Mount Carmel my goodness what an experience this turned out to be this was now Wednesday what a holiday this was turning out to be. I was sent to a secure wing all the doors were locked I could see the bright sunshine outside but here I was stuck in this prison. Here I met a really nice nurse her name was Margo she spent a lot of time with me. I was given a bed at the top of a ward there were six other patients there I just got a bed at the top of the room under a window with no locker and no light.

What a group of poor people were here there was nobody to have a conversation with and the routine was very rigid I was just beginning to get longer periods of normality the shower room was only open for an hour in the morning there was no doors the staff just watched everyone the toilets also had no doors and there was an old pillow case hanging on a nail to dry your hands I also remember my bed covered in ants as it was under the window how did I end up here? I was still slightly disturbed but by the next day it was as if I had snapped out of the state I was in and then for me it was so hard with my medical knowledge of how to act in a psychiatric hospital if I did things they would think I was manic and if I did nothing would they think I was depressed. I saw and heard many things in that place that shocked me.

Alasdair came to visit every day and would spend most of the day with me I would be in bed by seven pm as I had no light over my bed and there was nothing else to do. I still continued to read the bible every day and then I started helping to clean and to wash dishes in the kitchen at least it passed the time. I asked Margo on Friday if she thought I had come right she said I had and I asked her if I could get out she told me that it was a public holiday and the doctor was not in but would be in on Saturday.

Early Saturday morning I was again reading the bible and I was reading in $2^{ND}$ Timothy and especially chapter four "the time of my departure is at hand I have fought the good fight finished the race and kept the faith and finally there is laid up for me the crown of righteousness which the Lord the righteous judge will give to me on that day" I knew at that minute that I was saved and that I would always be cared for in this life and the life to come. What an experience and what a marathon I had run but it was all worth it.

Alasdair arrive later in the morning I told him I was getting out he asked who had said I told him I had not seen the professor yet but I told him about the reading and that I knew. One whole week of the holiday was gone but it did not matter I was now well again I remember getting out and heading for a decent meal the food had been terrible. I had to continue with the cardiac medication until I got home I suffered from headaches but enjoyed what was left of the holiday we had many chats about the last ten days Alasdair confirmed that he had known the whole time that I was on a spiritual journey I was reflecting on how God had planned this to perfection if this had happened in the UK I probably would not have nursed again I had this amazing experience in such an amazing biblical place he sure does work in very mysterious ways. We did return to Malta a few years later and visited all the hospitals that I had been to the only one that I was very familiar with was St Lukes the place where I had the out of body experience

We enjoyed the last week of the holiday the weather was beautiful and there was much to see and it was very interesting. I was absoloutly fine now but I was still a little fragile from the whole experience I was always afraid that I would go back to that state again but it has never happened. Alasdair had been in touch with my family and they were obviously very concerned about me but delighted that I was now well again. I was strangely at peace with myself I knew I had gone through a very amazing experience and I was buzzing.

# CHAPTER 12

After getting back to the UK I went back to work the next week I did not know what to expect from my colleagues and strangely not one of them mentioned any of what had happened at the course how strange was that! I still think that is amazing but nobody said a word. Of course Rhoda knew all about it and what had happened while I was away being a Christian herself she knew what it was all about she told me that I looked like a new person and I suppose I was. The very next day Iain the chaplain arrived on the ward Rhoda had informed him of what had happened before I left to go to Malta he was beaming and told me that he knew long before that something spiritual was going on in my life. He listened as I told him the story of what happened in Malta he said I was like Saul of Tarsus on the road to Damascus what an experience. Iain shared with me then his own equally amazing experience when he himself was converted. What amazing things happen to us to make us believe. Rhoda was telling me I should write a book about it I told her I would one day and here I am she said "you will forget" I told her no way how could anyone forget this it is now thirteen years ago and it is as clear to me now as it was then.

The first week back I started to go to church we went to the APC church as Alasdairs two sisters were attending there we had not been going since we came to Inverness I think Alasdair would have gone but did not go as I was not attending. It was also at this time that Alasdair revealed to me his own personal verse in scripture that spoke to him years before when he lost his wife and meant so much to him. The verse was in Philippians chapter 4 verse 19 "my God shall supply all your need according to his riches in glory by Christ Jesus" he equally knew then that he was always going to be cared for too. This verse was his comfort throughout his life since.

Life continued and was busy with life and work I continued studying and there were many late nights trying to finish assignments and working full time but I persevered I used to travel to Glasgow every few months which was a four hour drive to attend study days but it was all worthwhile I did eventually achieve my goal I now has a BSC in cancer and palliative care. What a proud day that was when I attended my graduation in Edinburgh with Alasdair by my side who had helped and encouraged me all the way and I did have tears on my cheeks to me it was way beyond anything I had ever dreamed of just shows what determination can achieve.

I continued to attend church and was getting much out of it. In the island where I grew up and indeed in this church that we attended the culture was that it was such a big event to take communion it consisted of a ritual communion only took place twice a year and if you wish to partake and take communion you have to go in front of the minister and elders and justify why you wish to take communion. Who am I to say how it should be done but I think this is a very very special thing and should be open to anyone who wishes to do so I do not think anyone has the right to judge anyone else. I personally think this ritual has kept many real genuine Christians from taking communion but that certainly does not mean that they are not saved.

Anyway during one communion a few years later I was attending church on the eve of the communion and one of the elders was preaching I was cruising along but during this service the preacher was saying that if there was anyone here tonight that knew that they were saved and were not going to the Lords table on Sunday that they were guilty of betraying the master I was rooted to my seat I had no intention of going but how could I not after hearing this powerful sermon I felt it was just for me. I stayed and went before the elders and told them why I wanted to take communion I was very emotional and tearful that was how big a thing it was.

So I took communion that Sunday the preacher was reading from the book of Kings chapter 8 and anyone who has a King James version of the bible look at the heading on the page "victory over Mount Carmel" oh my goodness if you remember that was the name of the hospital in Malta where it all happened for me. That to me was the icing on the cake I knew then that it was right and this was a real perfect sign that is was now all complete it was as if the Lord was cementing my faith I did not have any doubts and I still don't that that was very special. As I continue to grow in faith amazing things still happen to reinforce this. Alasdair never did take that step he did not take communion in Scotland I know it was because of the ritual that was involved and the deep tradition of the culture as I have said before it has kept many from taking this step but Alasdair took communion with me many times later in years to come and I do not think he was any less of a Christian because of that.

## CHAPTER 13

As cited before ever since I met Alasdair he would never stop talking about New Zealand he had been in the merchant navy when he was younger and had worked for New Zealand shipping and had spent many years there. In fact his intention was to emigrate to New Zealand and had actually bought his flight but did not go through with it in the end. Of course someone was looking after him as well and that was not the path he had to take. One of his friends from New Zealand always kept in touch and had actually visited him twice in Inverness. Alasdair always told me that when he retired that he would take me there and I could see for myself.

So true to his word in April 2004 we were heading to New Zealand we came out for four weeks I loved it immediately it was exactly as he had said a very amazing country with very amazing people. I met another four of his friends that were with him at sea and it was as if they had seen each other last week and it was now over forty years that is special and that is real friendship. We loved every minute of that holiday Alasdair always spoke of his lifelong dream to have lived there and I could see why. Well we loved it so much we came back in 2006 again in April and we loved it even more Alasdairs friends wife was a nurse and she tried to talk me into coming back to work for a year I was very tempted and I seriously looked into it after coming back but I thought it was too big a step to take and it was too far away.

Anyway within the following year Alasdairs nephew had emigrated to New Zealand with his work and was living in Wellington we had planned to go on a cruise that year but Alasdair was saying oh lets go to New Zealand one more time we will take my sister with us and she can also see her son and the children and also see this great country as well. I gave in eventually so off we went again this time it was at New Year and the middle of summer we were out in the Bay of Islands for a week on a friends boat and even crossed the ditch to Australia for the weekend I loved it so much that we made the decision then that we would come and stay. So back to the UK at the end of January and I started the ball rolling and discussed it with my family. In the end it was my son that nailed it for me he said "go Mum if you don't you will always regret it after all you are only 24 hours away in an emergency"

I decided to take a year sabbatical from my job in the Uk just in case it did not work out so that I could return there and have a job to go back to. I applied for nurse registration in New Zealand and started applying for a visa. I decided to sell my house in Inverness as I thought it was time to move on anyway I would put the money in trust and see what would happen if I returned then I would buy somewhere else. I also thought I would sell the furniture as it was cheaper than putting it in storage or to transfer it to New Zealand. Alasdair kept his flat and rented it to a friend.

As I was awaiting my visa I was looking on the internet at jobs I could not get my visa until I had a permanent full time job. Our desire was to come to Hawkes Bay as our friends were here there did not appear to be any jobs at this time I did not want to take any job my passion was cancer and palliative care. I came across an advert in Northland at North Haven hospice which appealed to me. I emailed to submit my interest in a job and explained that I was very interested but still awaiting my visa. I sent my CV and back and fore came emails one morning as I was finishing a night shift in the UK I got a phone call from the team leader. I was offered a 12 month contract how exciting. We also had friends in Northland so it was all good.

My house was put on the market and I sold my furniture I bought my house eleven years previous and I got back over three times what I had paid for it I think that I knew deep down that if it worked out in New Zealand that we would stay longer. Anyway everything was in place for us to go and start our adventure we left the UK in August 2007. It was sad to leave my job it had been part of my life for over fifteen years and I had very special times there and what a send off they all gave me. There was a recreation hall at the hospital they had hired it out we had a great night lots of food a live band all my friends and my family had also travelled to be with us I was showered with gifts from friends and even patients We were showered with good wishes and was presented with a beautiful jade necklace from the ward staff that I still treasure dearly. While on the subject of jades I must tell you another story about a jade the last time we were in New Zealand on holiday we were with our friends in Northland and we were getting ready to leave. My friend took me to the bedroom and told me she had something to give me as she thought I was special she told me she wanted to give me a jade which was carved from a family stone she was part Maori. She placed the piece of jade in the palm of my hand and then put her own hand over it and rubbed it. She then told me to put it on a chain and to wear it round my neck at all times.

On the last working day in the ward I was with another nurse when we heard a noise and on looking down we saw the jade on the floor could not understand how this had happened the chain was still round my neck and not broken. The nurse that was with me was a very spiritual person she told me that she was going to ask a very special friend of hers about it. When she came back the next day she told me that the woman had said "tell Christina that she does not need to wear that jade again it has now done its job and she is now going back to her roots" I never understood what that was about I did discuss it with my friend in New Zealand later the woman who gave it to me she just laughed I have never worn it again but still have it with me to this day.

# CHAPTER 14

We arrived in New Zealand in August 2007 to start our adventure our friends from Hawkes Bay came to meet us in Auckland we did not know they were coming they were delighted we were coming to stay but obviously disappointed that we were staying in Northland. We stayed with our friends in Northland for a few days until we settled and got over the jetlag I had a week before I started the new job. This was all so exciting although we had been together for many years we had never actually lived together before. Someone was looking after us within three days we were set up with a rental bought a car and bought furniture to start us off. We went into town the following day after arriving in the country we were looking in the window of real estate and out came the woman from the shop and asked us if we were looking for property she told us she had the perfect place that had just become available she told us she never did that kind of thing usually but something made her come outside. I think again someone was caring for us we got quite a nice home within walking distance to the hospice it even had a swimming pool.

Then without any of my knowledge the hospice had arranged a welcome for me along with another few new members of staff on the Friday this is what Kiwis do they had arranged it with my friends. I had already got to know some off the staff via email but had never actually met them. So off we went to the meeting Alasdair in his kilt and also our friends and along with another friend armed with his kilt and a set of bagpipes. What a welcome we got from everyone I immediately bonded with the place and the people and I had tears in my eyes as our friend played Amazing Grace on the bagpipes especially for me. It was as if I was just at home and not on the other side of the world as the lady said I was back to my roots and that was how it felt.

So I started work at the hospice the next week and I immediately became part of the family and that was just how it felt. I had never worked in a place that I was so welcomed and accepted I was happy and proud to be a part of it. We both loved everything about New Zealand just as Alasdair had told me Kiwis are very special people and of course the weather was amazing winter here is just like a summer in Scotland. We soon made friends with neighbours workmates and friends from church where we were readily accepted. After nine months we both knew we wanted to stay longer and decided to apply for residency. We had plans to go back at the end of the year anyway but we were coming back.

Why would we not come back we had both given up lots to look after our children and now it was our time. People who have never left the Island or indeed Scotland to live actually have no idea whatsoever they are steeped in the tradition and just go from day to day hey people there is another world out there go and discover it. I truly can not adequately describe what NewZealand is like you have to personally experience it for yourself to realise and everyone that has visited has said the same you have to see it for yourself they all say it is not what they expected

So we applied for residency I had all the points needed to stay in the country and Alasdair was allowed to stay as we were in a defacto relationship. We were delighted when we were granted the residency and we went back to the UK we were not sorry to come back and never once did we feel homesick or wished to be back in Scotland of course we missed people but never the country.

# CHAPTER 15

When we returned from the UK we bought a new home it was just built and was very nice Alasdair had sold his flat and I had collected the money from the trust from when I sold my house. The house was in a new sub division overlooking the golf course and was very nice with four bedrooms and two lounges we did not need such a big house but we thought it would be a good investment for the future. Alasdair had a great time landscaping the garden from scratch he was so happy it was such a change for him from sitting in a top storey flat in Scotland he was alive again he looked and acted years younger within a few months the garden looked amazing.

Alasdairs sister along with my best friend Rhoda had come to visit us while we were in the rental they were in New Zealand for three weeks and both loved it they could both understand how we lived here and we had a great time showing them round we even went to the south island great times. We continued living and enjoying life Alasdair said one day that he was going to see the doctor about a small spot on his back that he thought it was changing Alasdair had this small black spot on his back ever since I met him and looked just like a blackhead no bigger than that and was of no concern.

So he went to the doctor he told him that it was nothing to worry about and to come back to the surgery next week and he would remove it. Off he went one morning and he was taking longer than I expected he eventually returned and said that it was bigger that expected that it had been growing inwards and took longer there was quite a large wound there. The docter said that he thought it was still not anything sinister but he would send it to the lab anyway for pathology.

A few days later there was a phone call from the doctors that pathology was back and that he wanted to see Alasdair straight away I knew immediately that it was going to be bad news but did not anticipate how bad the news was going to be. Alasdair came back in tears he had melanoma grade 4 I could not believe what I was hearing we both knew how bad this could be and we were both gutted. I later found out that his mother had had a melanoma I was amazed he did not know this as it is essential to know what is family history if I had known maybe I would have forced him to have gone and seen about it earlier. Anyway we could not turn the clock back we had to deal with this as best we could.

This was the beginning of a long journey for Alasdair regarding his health he had been so well fit and healthy before this. Alasdair had a full body scan and that was normal no sign of any spread anywhere else. Alasdair spent thousands of dollars on private surgery for this he had a wide excision of the melanoma on his back then another biopsy on a mole behind his knee that was positive but a much smaller cancer then a wide excision of that then another biopsy of a mole on his belly that was benign. Then Alasdair had his first check up the consultant thought that he had felt a raised node in his left axilla so he sent him for an ultrasound scan that did not detect anything but picked up a raised node in the groin more worries. They tried taking an aspirate from that node but it was inconclusive so he had to have a sentinel node biopsy of that we waited for a week and danced when we heard that it was benign and all was well again.

It was at this time that I discussed with Alasdair what his wishes were if anything serious happened to him he told me he was happy to be in New Zealand we had the hard conversations and I made him make a will and I also updated mine at least that was dealt with and not a worry. We tried to be positive and not dwell on his illness but continued to live life to the full we went back to the UK almost every year to catch up with family not once were we homesick we were happy to be coming back to New Zealand every time.

# CHAPTER 16

I started walking with one of my friends after work each evening and I noticed that I was getting really breathless this was not entirely new but it was getting increasingly worse I had never experienced pain but the breathlessness was really bad at times. I thought that maybe it was due to the humidity in Northland but it was severe at times. Eventually I went to the doctor who referred me to the hospital I saw a cardiologist there who was really concerned when he gave me an exercise treadmill test my pulse shot up to over 200 in less than a minute. So he suggested that I have an echocardiogram and that was booked.

While awaiting this test one morning just getting ready for work I felt really light headed and a feeling of a weight on my chest and feeling as if I was going to faint I went in to work and immediately my friend Karen asked if I was ok that I looked terrible I told her my symptoms she said she was taking me to hospital to be checked out. I protested but she was not listening she said she was phoning Alasdair to meet us at the hospital and she took me in her car. I felt quite unwell in the car on the way which was a fifteen minute drive I was sweaty and felt a real weight on my chest i thought I was going to pass out.

We arrived at the hospital and Alasdair arrived as well I was seen immediately had bloods taken and had an ECG the registrar said straight admission to coronary care my head was spinning what was going on what a roller coaster. I was sent on a trolley upstairs not allowed out of bed and wired up to monitors the consultant came to see me and said that I was probably going on the helicopter down to Auckland to have angiograms I was gobsmacked. It was decided I would have an echocardiogram this was done and did not show any abnormalities so was decided that I would not go on the helicopter that I would go the next morning by road ambulance instead.

I continued to be monitored all the time and the nurses would come and ask if I had chest pain that my monitor was indicating that I did I said that I never had pain just a weight and heaviness thee next thing I was given GTN spray and this showed an improvement so the next thing I had an oxygen mask on my face and a GTN infusion I thought I was having a major cardiac event and I was lying there waiting for something bad to happen. My bloods came back I did not have a heart attack which was a relief. Something funny happened in amongst all this the consultant came round and asked if Karen was my daughter it became such a laugh that to us she became known as my Kiwi daughter and let me say now that she has lived up to that image she is such a good friend that she just feels like a daughter at times.

So next morning off to Auckland in the back of an ambulance still tied up to monitors which is a two hour drive Alasdair followed in the car I had the angiograms and that was all normal. I was discharged that afternoon but told not to travel back until the next day I was still shaken by the events of the last couple of days so we stayed in a motel overnight and drove back the next day. I took a week off work and I made an appointment to see a cardiologist privately. I still had no explanation of what had happened so this cardiologist gave me another exercise treadmill test same again a rapid pulse rate within a minute he did another echocardiogram and again no answer to anything I still continued to be breathless on excertion.

I went back to the doctor and told him I was no better and had exhausted all cardiac investigations he then sent me for lung function tests and again no abnormalities detected then he sent me to an ENT surgeon to rule out any abnormalities there again nothing so i told him if it would be worth trialing an inhaler so he gave me one it was like winning lotto it made a great difference although I never had asthma and my lung functions were ok but anyway I got relief which was great It was then that we decided that if it was the weather that was affecting me that we would move to Hawkes Bay where we always wanted to be.

# CHAPTER 17

We put the house on the market in June and thought it would sell straight away but the house market had crashed and it turned out to be a far bigger task than what we anticipated. I sent my CV down to the hospice in Hawkes Bay to see if there were any jobs I was told that they were not recruiting at present the next thing we heard was that the hospice was closing down following an audit that had taken place what a shock. Anyway we continued with our plans to move.

I was browsing jobs and came across a job at villa 6 at the local hospital it was in the chemotherapy suite this was what I had done for years in the UK and was more than qualified to do it but said to myself did I really want to do this again. I decided I would not apply and decided I would go on the casual pool at the hospital I had a phone interview and was accepted and was going down to Hawkes Bay in August for my orientation. We still had not sold our home and decided we would rent until we sold. In the meantime I saw the job at villa 6 came up again they had not appointed anyone so something was telling me that I should apply for it. So I did apply and I had a phone interview the week before I came down I went to meet them on the Monday and was offered the job three days a week Wednesday to Friday 8am to 4 30 yippee no more shifts so I agreed and we found a rental and moved to the Bay in August 2011

I started work in villa 6 and I felt at home from the beginning I met very special people but my heart was still in palliative care it never went away. Then the news came that the hospice was going to reopen and that the manager from Northland was coming for two years to set it up again my had they won the lotto if anyone could do it they had hit the jackpot this was a very special lady who had the essence of hospice in her heart I was delighted for them. I had met this woman a few times since she arrived in the Bay and she always asked when I was coming back to the hospice one part of me wanted desperately to go but I had just started this new job and I always thought there was some reason for it little did I know that very soon I was to discover what that reason was.

The week before Christmas that year I came home from work on Friday and Alasdair was sitting in the lounge looking very sad I asked him what was wrong then my whole world collapsed when he told me he had found a lump in his right armpit when he was in the shower. We both knew exactly what this meant the cancer had spread he had already made an appointment with the doctor. Alasdair saw the doctor and was referred to the hospital as I worked in the oncology clinic I told the consultant and he said phone him and tell him to come straight away So a needle biopsy was scheduled for the very next day how amazing the consultant came to tell me on the lasy day of the year that it was positive it was no shock to either of us what else could it be. I got a text from the manager at the hospice that evening wishing us a happy hogmanay she was devastated when she heard the news. So we went to our friends house that evening we went to the beach at midnight to watch the fireworks and we cried many tears beneath the stars all aware of the very uncertain future.

Alasdair saw the surgeon the next week and surgery was arranged in Wellington for the 17th of January for a total node clearance. Alasdair had a CT scan and it was all clear just one node affected which was the best possible result in the circumstances The manager at the hospice was in close contact and she said now that Alasdair had good news and when he had recovered from his surgery that I would then come and work at the hospice. The surgery went ahead and Alasdair made a good recovery one day at work I got a text if I was able to come to the hospice for an interview we are interviewing today I was flattered that she was wanting me to come and work for her I had discussed it with Alasdair and he always knew that was where I wanted to be and would support me in any decision I made. So off I went home changed out of my chemo scrubs and threw on a dress and went to the interview I was offered a job at the hospice and I started there in February 2011 I knew then that the reason for my job at villa 6 was so that Alasdair could get the best possible treatment and that he got everyone did all that they could for him.

# CHAPTER 18

I settled into hospice work again which is where I belong I felt at home again straight away our home in Northland still had not sold so we got a new agent we went to auction still did not sell but we got an offer after the auction which led us to put an offer on a house in Napier that we both liked but both fell through it was not meant to be. We continued looking and we saw a house in Hastings that we both loved it was an old villa but was nicely renovated we eventually had another offer for the house in Northland we decided to let it go someone got the best bargain ever we lost over one thousand dollars from what we paid for it but we decided to let it go and move on we bought the house in Hastings.

Alasdair had his follow up from his surgery they had decided to give him radiotherapy five weeks he had to travel to Palmeston North Monday to Friday and come home for the weekends he coped well with the treatment and we moved to the new house while he was having treatment. My friend Karen from Northland had visited us a few times since we moved then she also decided that she would also move down she had an interview at the hospice but at the last minute decided she would not go through with it. After I had been at the hospice for about six months they advertised for a team leader for the inpatient unit I was working in the community at the time. The manager asked me if I was going to apply for the job I told her no I did not intend to apply at all but each morning my daily readings which I do each morning were powerful. I was reading moments of peace for the morning thoughts and prayers to begin your day

How powerful those readings were I was reading that I needed to have confidence that God knows where he is leading you trust him do not fear what is ahead of you he will be with you every step of the way I could not ignore this it was very strong I was amazed. I went to speak to the manager and told her what was happening we prayed together and left it. I did apply for the job and had not heard anymore about it My friend Karen and her husband were coming down to visit two weeks later she was coming on Friday but she sent a text and said that they were coming on Thursday. I had not told her or anyone at work that I had applied for the job if I did not get the job I was not too bothered. Karen came at picked me up at work on Thursday of course we went to see the manager as we had all worked together in Northland she said oh Christina you have got your interview tomorrow good luck.

I told her that I had not heard anything oops she said did you not want Karen to know I told her that I had no information at all she then realised that it was genuine she went on the phone immediately she said we would cancel and get another date I said no we will just go ahead but you have a fifteen minute presentation to do I told her I would put something together. We think the letter for the interview had gone to the old address. Anyway is it not again amazing that Karen came down a day early and that she came to pick me up and we went to see the manager if not I would not have appeared at the interview that day he sure does work in mysterious ways I did get the job and started in that role

It was a challenge at the beginning but I trusted in a higher force and knew that for whatever reason I was meant to be there. Later Karen still had not lost her urge to come down to the Bay one morning I got a text from her asking if there were any jobs you wont believe it that very morning someone had resigned the job was advertised and Karen came down her husband also got a job and they moved down in August. We were all delighted and they became even closer friends Karen had not been feeling well for a while but she was now very much better we all knew she was capable of much more then the nursing services leader resigned and Karen was encouraged to go for the job.

I was delighted I knew she would be great I had worked with Karen for years and we sang from the same sheet and I told her I would support her in any way I could my goodness how things had changed in a short time who would have thought three of us from hospice Northland all working together in the hospice in Hawkes Bay there is a reason for everything. Karen and her husband became very good friends and we spent many happy hours together.

# CHAPTER 19

Alasdair spent a lot of time in the garden he took down a lot of old trees and built a picket fence at the front he also built a fence at the back and also a garden house he was happy doing this I had been wanting to get a little dog for some time Alasdair was saying we had to wait until the garden was secure so that a dog could be safe. I was looking on the internet and I saw a little dog that would be just perfect it was eight months old a black poochon which is a cross miniature poodle/bichon he was for sale as the family were moving to Wellington and were going to be renting and could not take the dog. We went to see him and we both fell in love with him immediately we took him home with us that day his name was Jolly. It was as if he had been with us forever he was so at home from the beginning and he followed Alasdair around like a shadow what a character he was

Shortly after this Alasdair went for routine blood check as he was on thyroxine for an underactive thyroid his counts came back low which was unusual they increased the dose but again his count had not increased. I was starting to get worried at this stage that something was wrong but did not think it was related to the melanoma and the doctor thought it might be some bowel problems. Alasdair had been losing some weight but he was working hard and again I did not think it was anything to worry about.

I was again getting breathless the inhaler did not seem to be doing much anymore so I made an appointment and got referred to a specialist. Then out of the blue I got a rash across my belly blow me I had shingles so I had treatment for that If that was not bad enough I started to have abnormal bleeding was referred to another specialist I needed to have a hysterectomy I was falling to bits. I saw the cardiologist and he started me on beta blockers quite a high dose it did make some difference but not a great deal I was to see him again in a few months.

 Before the winter came we had planned to put a roof on the decking to provide some shelter a friend was going to do the work and we ordered the wood it was in the garage and Alasdair was going to paint it. Alasdair was back and fore from the doctor and he seemed to be getting worse he now had swollen legs he had nausea and was getting really tired he started to prepare the wood and was really struggling. I was realising now that something serious was going on Alasdair was referred to a specialist but nothing was happening.

 I told him to go back to the doctor but he was saying to just wait as I was seeing him getting worse I made an appointment myself and went with him I knew deep down that it was serious but at the same time hoping that it was not. I said to the doctor that I wanted him admitted I said to him just tell me what I need to do and I will do it even if I have to call an ambulance The doctor phoned the hospital and Alasdair was admitted in three days time.

 I took the day off and went with him when he was admitted on the Tuesday he had some tests and a CT scan was booked for Thursday morning. The consultant told us that his symptoms could well be related to his cancer we both knew this and would not be any real surprise to either of us. The CT scan was done on Thursday morning and we had to wait until the afternoon for the result it was a very long day. I will never forget that moment when we got the news I knew deep down already what the result was going to be but when you actually hear the words it becomes final. The consultant and the registrar came into the room and I knew straight away by the manner what the news was going to be. The consultant broke the news very well which in my experience not every doctor is capable of doing he was on his knees by the bedside and told Alasdair that the cancer had spread to the stomach and the bowel and there was nothing that could be done. We both knew what that meant the consultant said that the only way to make certain that it was the melanoma was to do a biopsy via a scope. Alasdair said that he wanted this done as it would be closure for him this was planned for the next day and he also needed to have a blood transfusion as his count was low.

 We were both in tears we both knew exactly what this meant time was short for Alasdair. I took Alasdair home for a couple of hours we needed some privacy to get our heads round this what a welcome Alasdair got from Jolly he was so glad to see him he had been away for three days. Alasdair asked me straight "how long have I got?" he knew I would be honest with him I told him if he continued to deteriorate like he had in the last four weeks then that he had weeks and probably not months to live. I asked him what he wanted to do I knew he wished to be buried in Scotland I told him that I would support him in any way I could in any decision he made and that I would be beside him every step of the way no matter what I told him that I would do anything for the man that I loved unconditionally.

# CHAPTER 20

I told Alasdair that I did not care what it cost I would take time off work and that I would be there for him and that he would never suffer as long as I was able to care for him. I knew that he trusted me and believed in my ability to support him although this was my nursing speciality it is very different when it is your own but also at the same time I have said so often to so many people who question me as to why I was in terminal care and I continue to say so that it is a privilege and an honour to be part of the final journey of peoples lives nobody can change the situation we can only help to make the journey the best it can be and it is natural it is coming to us all no matter what.

I took Alasdair back to hospital that evening the next morning he had the scope and the biopsy done and was transfused two units of blood the consultant told him that there was no doubt at all in his mind that it was the melanoma from what he saw on the scope. We came home that evening and further talked and we decided that we would go home to Scotland while Alasdair was still able to travel safely. Alasdair then became fixated on getting home. The next day Saturday my friend Karen came and we went to the travel agents we booked a flight home business class for the following Tuesday. I phoned Alasdairs sister that night and thank goodness her son Peter was with her I told her the news and the plan and they would tell Alasdairs daughters it was too emotional for us to do. Peter was very close to Alasdair he had become a father figure as he himself had lost his dad when he was eleven years old they loved each other dearly and I had grown to love him also I had got on great with him since I first met him and he was very much like Alasdair in many ways.

We booked flights to London we would stay in London overnight and then travel up to Inverness the next day Alasdair had his daughter and four sisters living in Inverness and his wife was buried there. It did not give us much time but we managed to throw things together for the journey. News travelled and friends got in touch they all wanted to come and say goodbye to Alasdair before we left. We both could not believe the kindness, support and genuine love of all our friends and my workmates in New Zealand we were both deeply humbled and nothing was too much trouble. People started arriving with food and gifts food all cooked and ready to eat and genuine offers of anything they could do to help I genuinely believe that nowhere else in the world would this kind of support happen we only knew those people for a short time all they would say was "that is just what Kiws do" I feel so blessed to be part of this Kiwi family words can not express how amazing they all are.

My manager and her family were going to look after Jolly which was a huge relief. We visited the GP before we left he was shocked at the outcome but was so helpful you wont believe this but he had worked in Raigmore hospital and also at the highland hospice and also spent time at the GP practice that we were with when we were in Inverness what are the chances of all that! So he arranged everything and sent letters ahead to Inverness and he also prescribed medication for all eventualities if anything went wrong on the flight. Also the palliative care consultant came to visit us at home twice and she was equally amazing and she also knew the consultant at the highland hospice everyone was amazing and did all that they could for us to get home.

Friends started to gather and on the Monday night before we left thirteen of our dear friends sat round the table and had a meal they had come from afar as Northland and Wellington. They all said goodbye to Alasdair and it was all very emotional and we even had our friend playing the bagpipes. Alasdair said farewell to them all and he said that nobody was to come to the airport the next day it was all too hard for him he just wanted Karen and her husband and nobody else.

We set off for the airport the next morning this was the hardest and most emotional journey that we had ever made leaving the house knowing that Alasdair would never see it again he was so brave. When we got to the airport my manager arrived and we all had a cup of coffee together then she handed me three envelopes I opened them one was from hospice northland signed by many friends and contained money then a card from our hospice here again signed by friends and also containing money and another card from the manager and also lovely message and more money I had tears down my cheeks one thousand dollars in cash and genuine messages of love and support who else would have done this no wonder Alasdair always talked about the very special people that live in Nez Zealand and how genuine they all are.

My manager said to Alasdair that the hospice was lucky to have me and he replied that he knew that and that was why I needed to come back that I had much more work to do there yet. I knew I had to come back but did not know how I was going to be or what the future held then but I never forgot that. Then it was time for us to board the flight to take us on the first leg to Auckland I will never ever forget that walk across the tarmac boarding that plane and taking off from Napier knowing that Alasdair would never set foot on that land again it was tearing my heart apart and I wanted to scream I had a lump in my chest the size of a football and the tears were dripping off my chin. Neither of us could speak a word we just both held hands and had our own thoughts as that plane took off no words were needed we both understood what each others tears meant to us both. This was the hardest journey I ever had to make I was very emotional and it was Alasdair who was actually consoling me he was so brave and strong and as always the gentleman always thinking of others before himself.

Travelling business class was amazing and definitely the way to go if you can afford it and makes it even more difficult to travel any other way once it is experienced. Alasdair joked "look what I had to do to get you in to business class" at least he had not lost his great sense of humour. We eventually arrived in London safely and we stayed there overnight we were both exhausted both physically and even more so emotionally Alasdair was so pleased to be in the country I said to him that we were not home yet he replied that it did not matter now we were in the country and that was all that mattered. I realised then how bad he must be feeling if he thought he could not have made the journey home.

# CHAPTER 21

The last leg of the journey from London to Inverness was made safely and we arrived at lunchtime on Thursday It was very emotional meeting all the family it was exhausting and emotional. The GP arrived that afternoon at the house how amazing it was all arranged from the other side of the world we did not have to do anything. A few days later the consultant phoned from the hospice and we went to see him there. It was arranged for Alasdair to have another blood transfusion the following week and his counts had dropped again and he was commenced on medication to stem the bleeding. It was very emotional for me going to the hospital and meeting all my old friends there where I had worked for so long I trusted them all and I knew he would get the very best care possible it is very different when you are on the receiving end of care.

I continued to care for Alasdair he only managed a couple of journeys out in the car he was getting very fatigued and was getting weaker by the day every day we spent together was precious and I was so glad he was spending time with his family. We all knew what the outcome was going to be me and Alasdair could openly talk about death and dying and that will always be a great great comfort to me we could talk about it and I know everything was according to his wishes He said to me that he did not mind if he had to go to the hospice if I was not able to care for him but deep down I somehow knew that everything was going to be well I knew someone was in charge of the situation and we would be blessed through it.

I talked often with Alasdair about dying he was not afraid at all he would "often the passage" from the bible that meant so much to him and we would read from my little book each morning you wont believe it but that text came up twice while we were at home and not only that but his sister when she heard it told us that that very verse was written in her bible that she had when they first got married how amazing! We talked about funerals and somehow my thoughts went to the chaplain at the hospital that had meant so much to me all those years ago Alasdair had only met Iain once but of course he had heard all about him from me I thought he would be the perfect man to take his funeral we had lost touch with the church in Inverness the minister was now retired and people had moved on.

So I got in touch with my good friend Iain I did not know then that he had moved on to another hospital but it did not matter meeting Iain again after over five years was as if I had only seen him yesterday that is what genuine good friends do. Iain came to visit and he was delighted to be involved but obviously sad of the situation. Iain spoke with Alasdair regarding his funeral he wanted psalm 23 sung in Gaelic and of course Iain was ideal as he spoke the language Alasdair was open with Iain regarding what was special to him and I knew that he would take it all on board and would do a special service.

Iain came to visit a couple of times Alasdair continued to deteriorate and was getting weaker and eating very little. Then a bombshell Iain was going on annual leave for three weeks he was going to the island for two weeks and then south for a week. I thought to myself that there was no way that Alasdair was going to survive for that time as I could see a steady decline. Anyway Iain came to visit on the Friday before he left and spent time with Alasdair as he was leaving he said to Alasdair "I will see you again my friend whichever side of life but I hope it is on this side you wait for me until I get back" Alasdair replied "I will try my very best" So Iain left for his leave I was sad but he had left a colleague at work to take over in his absence he was also a friend of mine he came to visit and spent some time with us.

So we continued day by day the hospice district nurses and GP were great support Alasdair continued to deteriorate and so easy to care for although it was very very hard emotionally to see a much loved man fade away. Not once did Alasdair ever show any bitterness or anger he was so accepting of everything and that in my experience only comes with faith he used to ask how long this was going to take in his head he was ready but the body was strong. Everything was in place when things deteriorated we had all the drugs we needed in the house we got a hospital bed and a special mattress to make Alasdair as comfortable as possible.

I will not pretend that this was an easy time for me but again one I had to go through because I loved Alasdair and would do anything that I could for him. It was not easy not having any of my family around me to support me on a daily basis as they all lived on the Island I did speak to them every day but it was not the same not having them around. I was a stranger in the home and surrounded by people that were never my family although welcomed it is never the same the exception was Alasdairs sister Peggy who I could sit down with and share everything she and Alasdair were very close and very like each other in nature. Every Saturday we used to go to lunch together so that I could have time out I will always treasure those times I love her dearly always did and always will.

As Alasdair continued to deteriorate and starting to struggle to swallow his medication it was decided to commence some morphine tablets as they were smaller and the equivalent of what he was already on it was a very small dose just 5 mgs twice a day. Well on day three it became evident that he was toxic from the morphine well that is what I thought or was it disease progression. I observed Alasdair was hallucinating and confused and could not sleep or relax. This was very disturbing for everyone I did consider if this was terminal restlessness which is common but I did not think Alasdair was quite there yet there was consensus that we should give some sedation to help him but I had a gut feeling that we should hang out and see what happened. We stopped the morphine and I stuck it out for three days with very little sleep but he did come right I am so glad to this day that we did not sedate him then once the morphine was out of his system he was fine again very weak and tired but completely lucid.

Then Peter phoned from New Zealand he was coming over to see Alasdair he became very emotional when he heard that he was coming they were always very close and very similar in nature. The same week my daughter also came over from the Island to see Alasdair as she was going to have major surgery on her knee the following week. Alasdair was very weak by now but he enjoyed having them to visit but what an emotional day when they both left on the Sunday saying goodbye was so hard knowing that they would never see each other again in this world we both cried buckets.

Alasdair was getting weaker was now not eating just having fluids and very weak The next weekend I could see signs that time was very short now he was experiencing pain in his legs and was showing signs of shutting down which is common and was now needing small doses to morphine to control the pain. The doctor came to visit on the Monday and it was decided that Alasdair needed to have a pump to control his pain as he was now unable to take tablets that was to be commenced on Tuesday morning. That afternoon I could see signs that confirmed to me that the end was near Alasdair was staring into the beyond I had seen this so often before alongside people that are dying I asked him what he was looking at he told me he was seeing the bright light he could see it then he said to me that he was now going to sleep. I thought he still had a day or two and was going to be unconscious and not able to communicate I told him it was fine to go to sleep that I would be there right beside him all the way.

# CHAPTER 22

That evening Iain knocked at the door on his way home from work he was back I had prayed so hard that this would happen he walked in and said to Alasdair "you waited for me" "yes I did said Alasdair" with tears in his eyes. There was lovely fellowship in the room that evening and was very special we all knew that Alasdairs journey was coming to an end. Iain read from the scriptures in John chapter 14 "in my fathers house are many mansions I go and prepare a place for you I will come again and receive you unto myself that where I am ye may be also" how powerful that was and I think cementing the journey for Alasdair. Iain told him how he had prayed every day while he was away that he was still alive and told him that he went with his family and had a picnic in North Tolsta in his honour this is where Alasdair was born and brought up.

Iain told me that he knew that Alasdair was going to wait for him he just knew amazing faith and Gods plan again. As I spoke with Iain at the door as he was leaving he said to me that in his fifteen years as a hospital chaplain that he had never met anyone with such grace and dignity facing death. I said to Iain "he is a very special man" his reply was "but you are a very special woman I think you are equal" For me Alasdair lived his life a true genuine gentleman and faced death in the same way with his gentle quiet faith he was at peace and that was evident for all to see.

That evening I tucked Alasdair in as usual and have him a drink of cold water I wished him a good night he replied the same in Gaelic and we went to sleep. In the early hours of the morning of August 14 2012 I heard a gasp I turned on the light Alasdair had taken his final breath I have over the years seen many people pass but nothing like this he looked as if he was sleeping and looked like a porcelain doll I did not need to touch him his journey in this world was over no more suffering. Of course I was very sad we all knew the outcome but when it actually happens you are never prepared. I was sad his journey on earth was over but also look forward to when we meet again if there is such a thing as a good death then this was it.

I woke up Alasdairs daughters It was 04 45 in the morning there was no rush to do anything we spent some time together. We contacted the family to inform them and I phoned New Zealand to let them all know that Alasdairs journey was over. I lit a candle by the bed and opened the little book at the page with the reading that meant so much to Alasdair "my God shall supply all of my needs according to his riches in glory by Christ Jesus" and placed it beside the candle. We were all sitting in the lounge I asked what the time was we looked round the clock had stopped at 04 40 my heart missed a beat. This was Alasdairs own clock he had given it to his daughter to look after when we came to New Zealand and was a gift from his work when he left his job as a janitor at the local school years before. My goodness the power of the holy spirit I believe this was the exact time that he passed away it was as if someone was saying that it was ok. It was a comfort but I knew that my life was never ever going to be the same ever again

We could not have the funeral for a week that is normal in a city but it is a very long time to wait. Alasdair was taken to the funeral parlour and was dressed wearing his merchant navy tie that meant so much to him he had never stopped talking about his days at sea and especially New Zealand. I am so pleased that eventually he got his wish to live there it meant so much to him he used to tell everyone that he had achieved everything on his bucket list while he was living here the last five years of his life I just wished it had been longer. It was a huge commitment but I am so proud and happy that I was able to make it happen for him and made his dream a reality. Alasdair had now completed his final journey

> I am standing upon the seashore a ship at my side
> spreads her white sails to the morning breeze
> and starts for the blue ocean. She is an object
> of beauty and strength and I stand and watch her
> until at length she hangs like a speck of white cloud
> just where the sea and the sky come down to mingle
> with each other. Then someone at my side says
> "There—shes gone"

Gone where? Gone from my sight—that is all
She is just as large in mast and hull and spar
As she was when she left my side and just as able
To bear her load of living freight to the place of
destination. Her diminished size is in me not in her
and just at that moment when someone at my side
says "There shes gone" there are other eyes watching
her coming voices to take up the glad shout "There she comes"
And that is dying (Anon)

## CHAPTER 23

On Thursday my older sister phoned from the Island and said she was coming over she said to pack a bag that she was taking me to a nice hotel her treat she would be arriving on Saturday morning. What a kind and beautiful thing to do and was just what I needed. We spent quality time together reminiscing over past times anyone that knows or has met my sister will know how special it is to be in her company she is a real tonic and this was special. It had been a very stressful eight weeks and this was just what I needed time with my own family and was therapeutic to say the least. All my other family started arriving for the funeral and we all had a family meal on Monday night together.

Tuesday morning came and the day of the funeral which was to be the final hurdle. My dear friend Iain paid a very special tribute to Alasdair in a beautiful service over one hundred people attended some had travelled from the island and also friends from many places who all attended to celebrate Alasdairs life and pay last respects. To me it was as if it was all a dream and I was going to wake up—I wish. The day passed in a blur. That night I spent with my daughter in a hotel as I was going to travel with her the next day to the island to spend some time with my daughter who was just recovering from major surgery on her knee. I met up with friends and neighbours there which was very comforting and we talked about old times and the good memories that we shared.

When I was there for a week I knew I had to start making plans to go back to New Zealand I was not looking forward to the long journey on my own but what choice did I have. I knew it was Alasdairs wish that I would return he knew by then that I loved living there and also the very special friends that I had there his words to me were "why would you not go back"

61

there is no answer to that why indeed. There is no way I would ever go back to the Island of that I am absoloutly certain I have not lived there for over twenty years and those that have never left do not understand. Where else would I go Inverness holds no sentimentalities for me I worked there for many years but it has now changed so much and all my friends have now moved on. Of course Alasdair is buried there but to me that is just where his bones are resting I feel his spirit is here with me and I feel very close to him at times as if he is still with me and I know that he is.

 I took the step and booked my flight to return I would spend a couple of days in Inverness and then travel to Stirling to spend time with my son and his family prior to leaving for New Zealand on the 5th of September When I left the Island it was very hard my two daughters and Alasdairs daughter came to see me off it was not easy leaving. I spent time in Stirling my son took me to Glasgow airport that again was not easy.

 I arrived in New Zealand and was met by friends and I spent the night with them I would go back to the house the next day. My dear friend Karen had taken time off work and was going to stay with me and she was at the house when my friends took me back the next day. It was so hard to walk into the house on my own without Alasdair I knew that life would never be the same again and this proved it to me. I was so glad that my friend Karen was staying with me and then the next hurdle my little dog Jolly. How was he going to be my friends had him longer than we did we only had him for five weeks and they had him for over eight weeks but I needed have worried. My friend took him back that evening Jolly jumped out of his arms had a couple of sniffs and it was as if he had never been away what a welcome but he knew someone was missing and was looking for him for a long time one day he got into the car and would not leave the drivers seat I had to lift him out he must have been smelling him animals are so wise and sensitive.

 I was aware that Jollys birthday was close and that he needed a vaccination when he was one as I had given my friends his passport when they had him and when I got him back and looked at his passport I felt goosebumps from my toes to my head you wont believe it his birthday was the 14th of August the very day that Alasdair passed away what a special little boy this was he was so meant to be and a real treasure I don't think I would be here without him he is such a character great company and I feel very safe with him around.

 During the next few days I relaxed with my friend then I had to think about going back to work I decided I would take another week off to get over the travelling and would go back the following week. Friends came to visit and again so very kind and supportive on the Friday evening my workmates came round after work they came with wine and food and we spent time together so that really broke the ice and paved the way to make it easier for me to go back to work. Meeting people for the first time is overwhelming so I was pleased that I had already met some before I came back to work.

I was moping in the house my lounge was decorated in black and red I looked around that red colour was doing my head in for some reason I just had to get rid of it a friend at work later told me that red is the very worst colour to have around you when you are grieving and I believe it. So I got rid of the red colour I put wallpaper up on one wall and replaced all the red with blue and green it occupied my mind for a while. I also started planting in the garden friends had given a rose bush call in loving memory and Karen had given me a rose called love me do the hospice had given me a Kowhai tree which is the hospice symbol and I bought another rose called hawkes bay rose and planted that in memory of Alasdair from hospice Northland. I found working in the garden very therapeutic and comforting and always felt Alasdairs spirit with me there.

So back to work and everyone was so supportive what a special family to be part of I quess everyone that works at hospice are very special people anyway but I feel so blessed to be part of this wonderful organisation. The worst part of the day was coming home from work and Alasdair was not there to meet me he would always be there all organised starting the evening meal and all the chores done but Jolly was always there with a huge welcome. Life will never be the same again in time I will get used to it and it will become more bearable. That was Alasdairs time to leave this world I know he is in a better place I miss him so much and always will but I know we will meet again We both spent the best part of our lives together and who can forget that the precious memories are ingrained and nobody can take those away. I recorded Alasdairs funeral service and have it on CD and I watched it so often in the early days I would watch it and cry buckets tears are healthy and a great release. I was pretty low at times tears would come out of the blue when I least expected it like one day I was driving past the golf course where we had spent many happy hours together and I had to stop the car as I could not see through the tears.

## CHAPTER 24

It is still like that for me months later and will probably continue for many months to come that is grieving and has to be worked through it will evolve itself. I have not yet been able to remove any of Alasdairs belongings all his clothes are still hanging in the wardrobe all his drawers full I just get a comfort surrounded by his belongings Everything in the garage is just the way he left it all his hats hanging up his tools on the bench just the way he left them I know I will deal with it when the time is right there is no rush. I even collected his hair from the hair clippers I had cut his hair for years and I have that in cotton wool in a dish it is part of him mad maybe but it is a comfort to me.

Now it is time for me to deal with my own health issues it was now over five months since I knew that I needed a hysterectomy and also needed to see the cardiologist regarding my medication I had private insurance and my surgery was booked for November blow me they turned down my claim they said that because I knew before that I had fibroids that they were turning down my claim I was so disappointed and could not stop crying why was this happening to me I was now on the pulic system and had to wait months for surgery.

Then some amazing news my daughter Margaret and my granddaughter Chloe were coming to visit over Christmas and New Year I was so excited and could not believe it what a blessing and was just what I needed he sure does have a plan for everything. We had such an amazing time together and they both loved it immediately They both said that they now perfectly understood why I lived here and as I have said one has to see it for themselves to understand it. There was very emotional moments at New Year missing absent friends I was so happy they were with me my first Christmas together on my own. They met great friends and enjoyed the great weather I just wished they had stayed longer to see more of the country maybe next time. I hope they will be back and other members of my family too I was so sad when they left it is always hard saying goodbye

So back to work and busy with everyday living and looking forward to a cruise in April we had booked this a while ago Alasdair would not let me cancel it he said to take a friend with me in his place so I asked a friend from work to come along it will be sad because Alasdair could not make it but I am sure his spirit will be with us all the way. Out of the blue I got a phone call from the hospital my surgery was booked for 12 th March I was feeling much better now on my medication I was now on a high dose of beta blockers. Well you wont believe but the night before my surgery it was cancelled because the surgeon was not well why was I going through all this anyway surgery was booked for the following week.

The day arrived and all set for surgery Peter came from Wellington to look after the house and Jolly my friend Karen came and picked me up and took me to the hospital it was now all over I did really well and was home in three days now the long road to recovery I would be off work for six weeks Peter did some cooking and stacked the freezer Karen came to stay when Peter went home until I became more mobile.

So here I am now I am still in New Zealand this is the place I now call home oh of course I am sad and lonely at times I still cry at the drop of a hat but I would be sad and lonely anywhere in the world of course I miss having family around me but they have their own lives to lead and it is all the more special when we do meet and spend time together. Where else in the world would I have got the support that I have had over the last year nowhere not even in my own country. Kiwis are special people and I consider myself very blessed to have those people in my life. If someone had told me when I was younger that I would in my twilight years be living on the other side of the world and to have experienced everything that I have in my life I would have said "impossible" but it proves that life is set out for us and everything that happens in our lives is for a reason doors open and doors close but the long term plans are way beyond our plans we all have to walk the path set out for us and finish our journey as planned

# CHAPTER 25

If we follow Gods way and there is a way for everyone oh for grace to walk the path and the journey with wisdom and holinesss we may not travel business class but we will travel safely. "Then shall thou walk safely and thy foot shall not stumble" (proverbs chapter 3 v 23). I remember seasons in my life of labour trials and tribulations in which I received special strength that I wonder about. In sickness I was patient and in bereavement resigned God gives unexpected strength. In this world ye shall have tribulations (John chapter 16 v 33) we all have our own share of it he says be off good cheer I have overcome the world it is so hard to perceive when we are sorely tried but we must never lose sight of it. He will be our guide even unto death (Psalm 48 v 14) we all need a guide he knows the way and he will push us along until we reach our journeys end in peace. If we place ourselves under his guidance we will not miss the right path.

The comfort is that he is our God for ever and ever even beyond death when that crown of righteousness will be placed on our head what a day that will be this was the promise to me in Malta over thirteen years ago and means just as much and more to me today as it did then. Trials and tribulations since then as I have matured in years and in faith have added to my understanding of life. None of us can avoid adversity loss and hardship but we do have a choice in how we react and face it. Most people would say that they would not wish the bad experiences but agree that it did teach them about their own character and strengths. The act of faith is not a leap from darkness into light it is an affirmation that light exists beyond the darkness.

There is confidence when we know that if we trust in God whatever has happened in the past and whatever may happen in the future we have the promise that God will not forsake us and will safely keep us on the right path until our journey ends LIFE IS A JOURNEY and one day it will end for us all but rest assured there is life after death and that will be the most exciting journey of all I look forward to it do you?